国民抗戦必携

NATIONAL RESISTANCE MANUAL

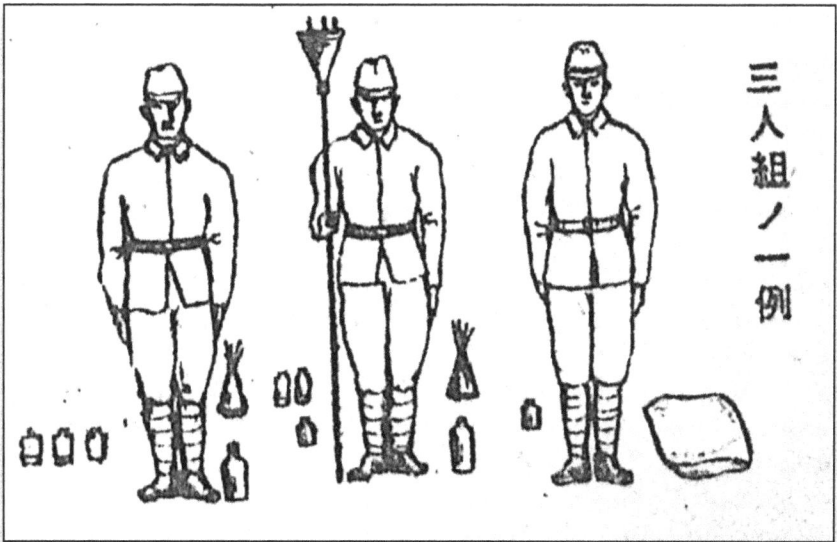

JAPANESE ARMY MANUAL

PUBLISHED 1945

TRANSLATED BY ERIC SHAHAN

Translator's Introduction

國民抗戰必携

一億特攻

本土決戦の手引き

Translator's Introduction

This is a translation the *Kokumin Kosen Hikkei* 国民抗戦必携 *National Resistance Manual* published by the Army Section of the Imperial General Headquarters on the 25th of April 1945. The manual contains 26 illustrated pages. Newspapers in Japan also published additional information to supplement the manual. Newspapers such as the Yomiuri and Asahi ran articles with just the supplemental information. However the Chubu Nihon Newspaper 中部日本新聞 published the entire *National Resistance Manual* over the course of 8 issues and included the additional information as well. This translation will include the complete *National Resistance Manual* as well as the information included in the 8 Chubu Nihon newspaper articles which ran from June 19th ～ 26th 1945.

Left: A June 10th 1945 Yomiuri Newspaper article announcing the forthcoming publication of the *National Resistance Manual* as well as *The People's Guide to Building Fortifications*. The article is titled, *100 Million Special Attack Soldiers : A Guide to the Final Battle in the Homeland.*

How the Chubu Newspaper articles were organized. This is article #3 from June 21st 1945.

These illustrations and the corresponding captions are pages from the *National Resistance Manual.*

The newspaper titled each section, which was not in the manual

National Resistance Manual

Article Number

This is the supplemental information not in the stand-alone manual.

JAPANESE ARMY MANUAL

NATIONAL RESISTANCE MANUAL
Published April 25th 1945
Newspaper Articles June 19th ～ 26th 1945

Newspaper Article 1
Directly Attacking Enemy Tanks Without Fear

A. Outline

A. Outline

If the enemy choses to attack the mainland, a combined force of 100,000,000 Tokko, Special Attack Soldiers, will obliterate them. They will, with absolute certainty defend this imperial land.

B. The *Kokumin Giyutai*, People's Honorable and Brave Unit, also known as Volunteer Fighting Corps, will conduct the training, build fortifications and teach everyone how to defend their locality. This will include how to advance on the enemy undercover and kill them. It is essential that all cooperate with the military's strategy.

C. The training necessary for this final battle is as follows:

    a. How directions will be issued from command

    b. How to be a sniper, throw grenades, cut down enemies with a sword and do close quarters attacks on tanks.

Newspaper Article 1
Directly Attacking Enemy Tanks Without Fear

Chapter 1
How to Do a Close-Quarters Attack on a Tank

How to Do a Close-Quarters Attack on a Tank

1. Essential data regarding enemy tanks and striking points.

The enemy tanks should be attacked in vital areas. The enemy Americans primarily use two types of tanks, the M4 Mid-sized tank and the M1 Heavy tank.

The best way to attack an M4 tank is to detonate a futon-bomb on the dome or on the back. The back of the tank can also be attacked with Molotov cocktails. The front of a tank as well as the turret are vulnerable to bomb-tipped spears as well as hand-thrown explosives. Hand-thrown explosives can shatter a tank's treads Charging at the advancing tank while holding a 7 kilogram quick-made bomb is also an effective method.

For the heavily armored M1 tank, attack the dome or back with a futon-bomb. Molotov cocktails can also be thrown at the back. Stab into the sides of the tank with bomb-tipped spears. Attacks to the front of the tank should be done with a 10 kilogram quick-made bomb.

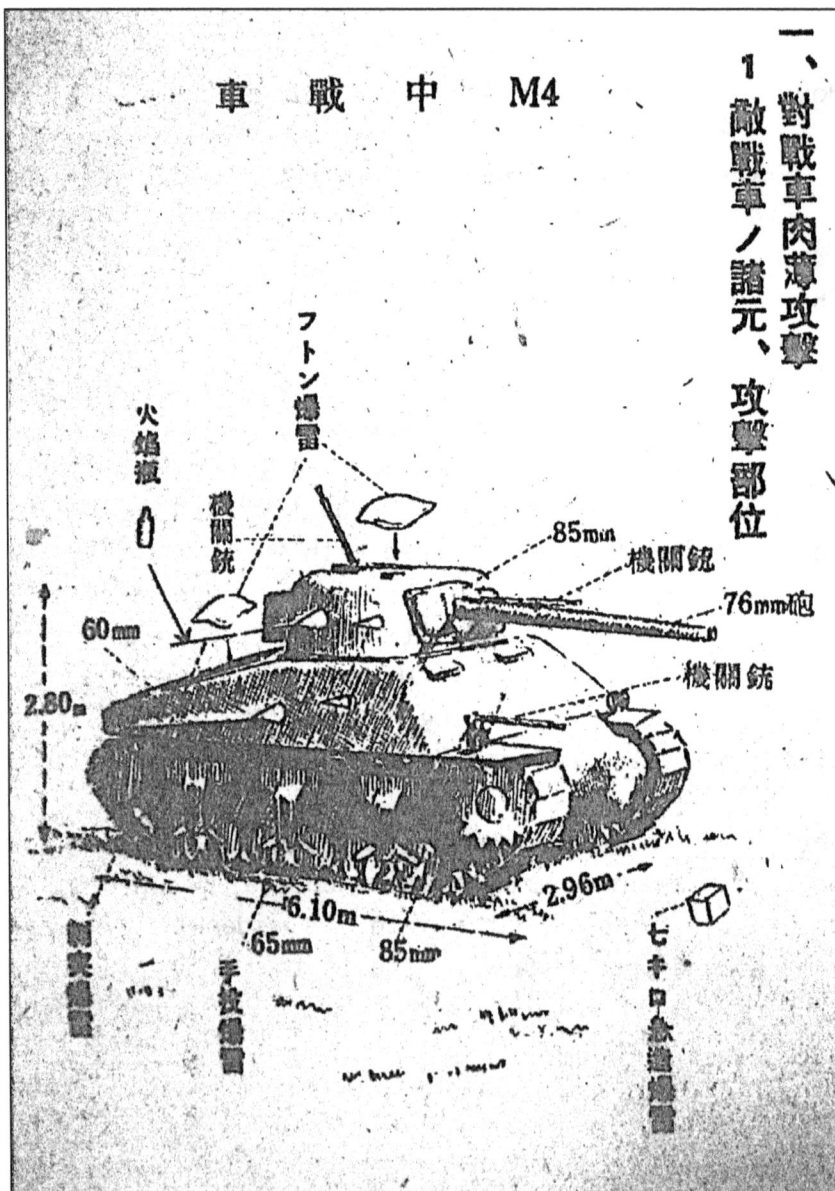

一、對戰車肉薄攻擊
1 敵戰車ノ諸元、攻擊部位

車 戰 中 M4

フトン爆雷
火焔瓶
機關銃
85mm
機關銃
76mm砲
60mm
機關銃
2.80m
6.10m
2.96m
65mm
85mm

M4 Mid-Sized Tank

6.1 meters long

2.9 meters wide

2.8 meters tall

The armor on the prime areas such as the front and turret is 85 millimeters thick. The weakest points are 60 millimeters thick. It is armed with a 76 mm cannon and 3 heavy machine guns.

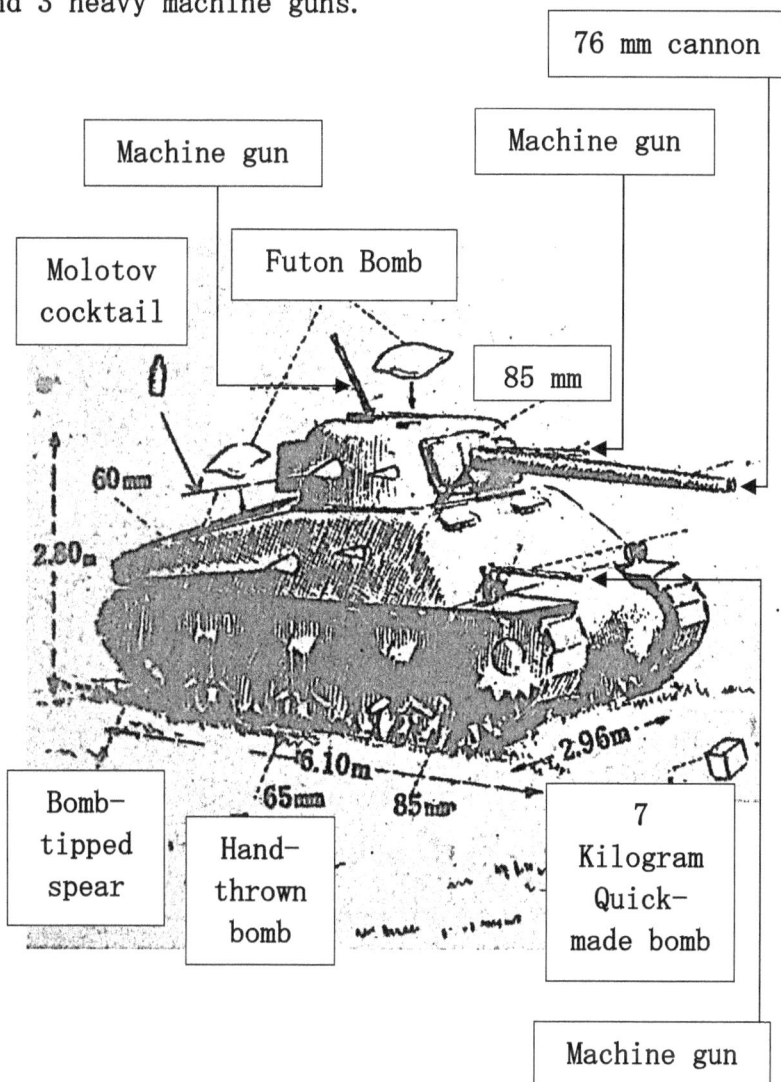

76 mm cannon

Machine gun

Machine gun

Molotov cocktail

Futon Bomb

85 mm

60 mm

2.80m

6.10m

2.96m

Bomb-tipped spear

Hand-thrown bomb

65 mm

85 mm

7 Kilogram Quick-made bomb

Machine gun

車　戦　重　M1

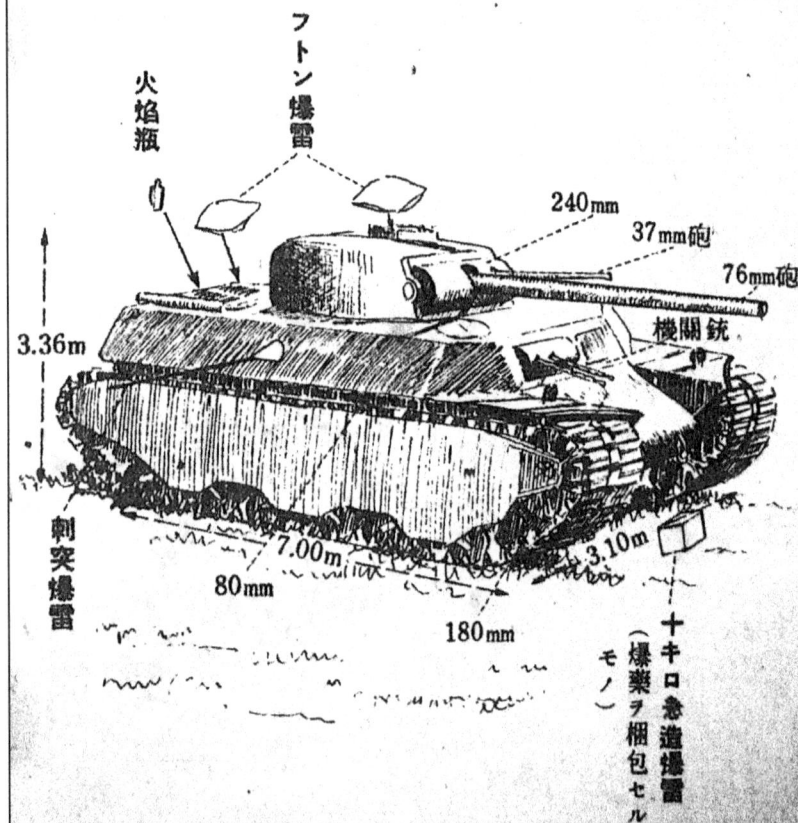

火焔瓶

フトン爆雷

240mm

37mm砲

76mm砲

機關銃

3.36m

刺突爆雷

7.00m

80mm

180mm

3.10m

十キロ急遭爆雷
（爆藥ヲ梱包セル
モノ）

M1 Heavy Tank

7 meters long
3.1 meters wide
3.36 meters tall
Armor is 24-80 millimeters thick.
It is armed with one 76 millimeter cannon and 1 37 mm cannon and carries two heavy machine guns.

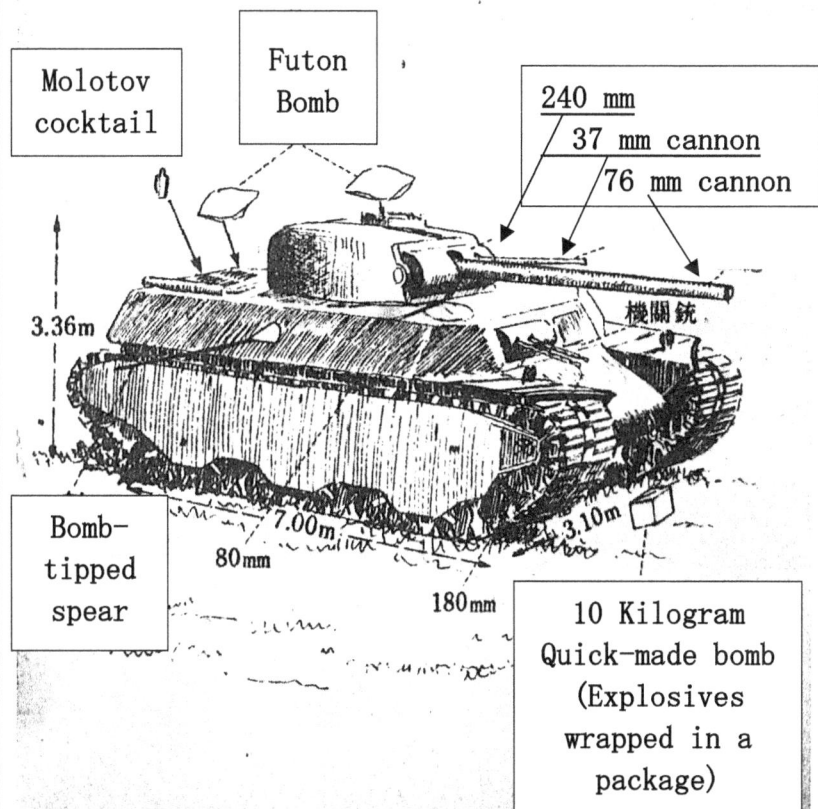

Molotov cocktail

Futon Bomb

240 mm

37 mm cannon

76 mm cannon

機關銃

3.36m

Bomb-tipped spear

7.00m

80mm

180mm

3.10m

10 Kilogram Quick-made bomb (Explosives wrapped in a package)

Newspaper Article 1
Directly Attacking Enemy Tanks Without Fear

2. The Strategy Used by Enemy Tanks: Advancing

2. The Strategy Used by Enemy Tanks: Advancing

Looking at the standard operating procedure of the enemy American military, tank units tend to send scout troops ahead. The foot-soldiers assigned to accompany an M4 tank will form in ranks to the sides and advance forward slowly, firing at any essential target they come in contact with.

Stationed behind that unit the M1 tanks continually fire on the essential targets similar to how the soldiers that are assigned to stationary artillery operate. Either of these targets are delicious treats for us.

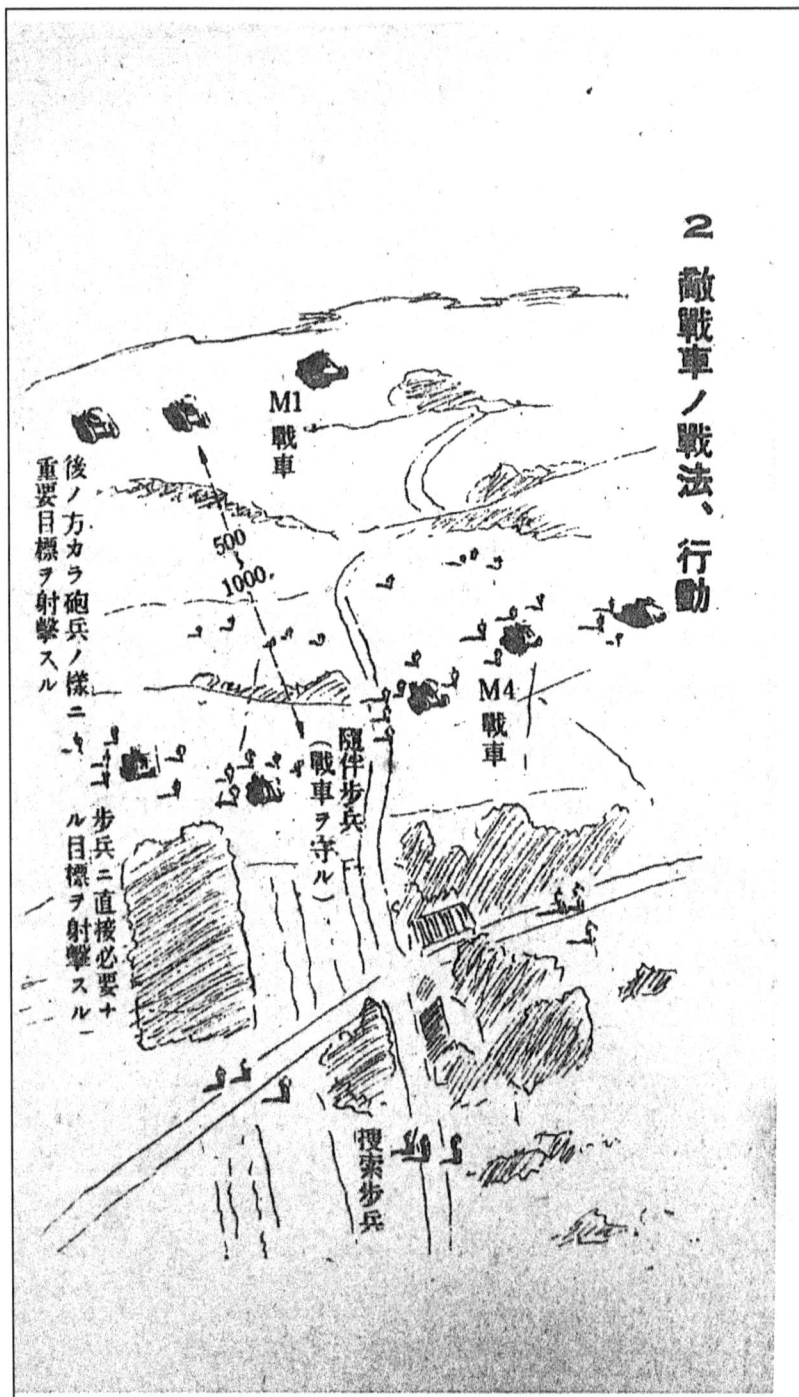

2. The Strategy of Enemy Tank Units and How They Move.

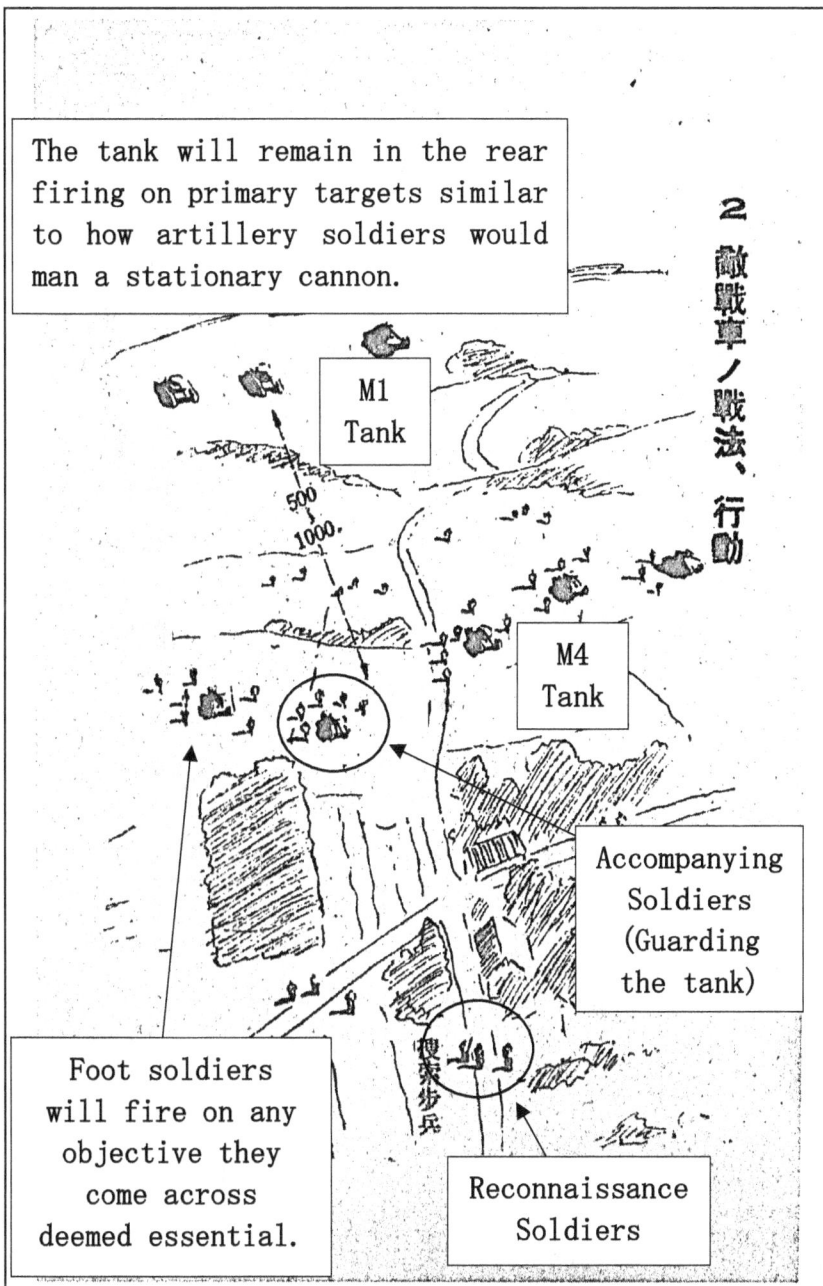

The tank will remain in the rear firing on primary targets similar to how artillery soldiers would man a stationary cannon.

2 敵戦車ノ戦法、行動

M1 Tank

500
1000.

M4 Tank

Accompanying Soldiers (Guarding the tank)

捜索歩兵

Foot soldiers will fire on any objective they come across deemed essential.

Reconnaissance Soldiers

Newspaper Article 2
Well-Practiced Volunteer Attack Units

3. Information on How to Conduct Close Quarters Attacks and How to Form Units

國民抗戰必携 ②

練磨の挺身攻撃

3 肉薄攻撃資材 と組の編成

4 攻撃實施

5 對戰車肉薄攻撃 の支援

1 手投爆雷 (安全栓ヲ抜ク) 火焔瓶

2 割突爆雷

3 フトン爆雷

手投爆雷　安全栓

割突爆雷

4 フトン爆雷　三人組ノ一例

2 火焔瓶　命中時果　戦車ノ板ニ横ノマンツケル

鋼線　突スイッチ　瞬間発火

3. Information on How to Conduct Close Quarters Attacks and How to Form Units

One method we have for attacking and destroying the American supply chain strategy that provides material resources their military is our willingness to throw our bodies at them and cut our enemy down. This is due to our utter devotion to defending our country. This is our *Tokko Senpo*, Special-Attack War Strategy.

The resources for a close-quarters assault on tanks are as follows:
1. *Tenage Bakurai* : Hand-Thrown Explosives
2. *Kaenbin* : Fire Bottles (Molotov Cocktails)
3. *Shitotsu Bakurai* : Bomb-Tipped Spears. A bomb that explodes on impact when you charge a tank and stab it like you are attacking with a spear or bayonet.
4. *Futon Bakurai* : Pillow Bomb. A device that will ignite 10 seconds after you pull the safety pin. Another version is a parcel of explosives called a *Kyuzo Bakurai*, Ready-Made Bomb. Also known as a Jirai, Mine.

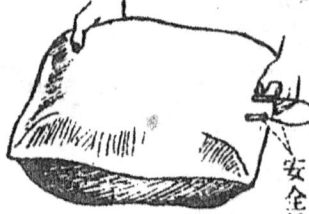

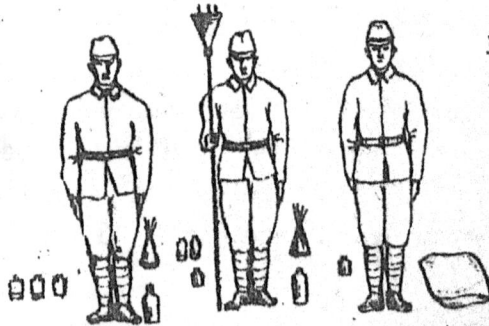

３　肉薄攻撃資材、組ノ編成

１　手投爆雷

安全栓

拔ク

２　火焔瓶

命中時發火

安全栓

戰車ノ板ニ横ノマ、ブツケル

３　刺突爆雷

安全栓

銅線（ソノマ、突ク）

突イタ瞬間發火

４　フトン爆雷

安全栓

引拔ク十秒後發火

三人組ノ一例

其他爆藥ヲ梱包シタ急造爆雷、地雷等ガアル

3. Information on How to Conduct Close Quarters Attacks and How to Form Units

2. Molotov Cocktail Throw it sideways like this onto the tank's armor plate.	1. Hand-thrown Explosive Ignites when it strikes the target.

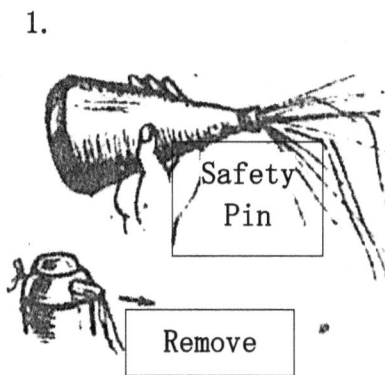

2.

1.

Safety Pin

Remove

3. Bomb-Tipped Spear

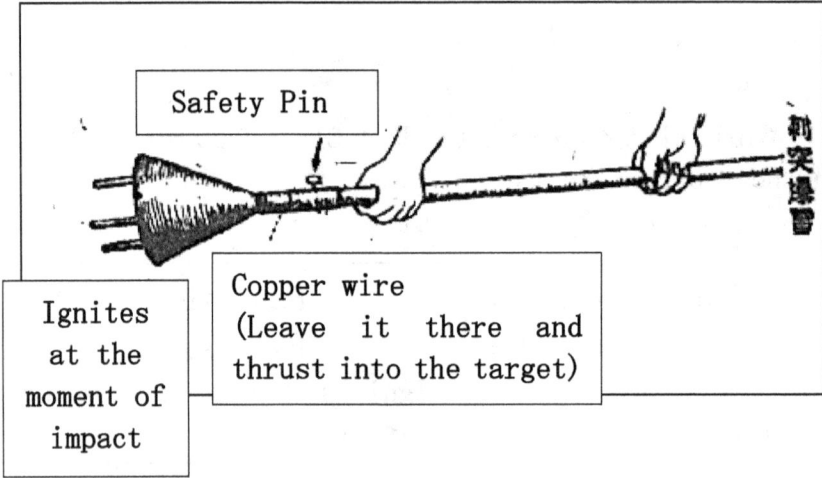

Safety Pin

Ignites
at the
moment of
impact

Copper wire
(Leave it there and
thrust into the target)

4. Futon "Pillow" Bomb

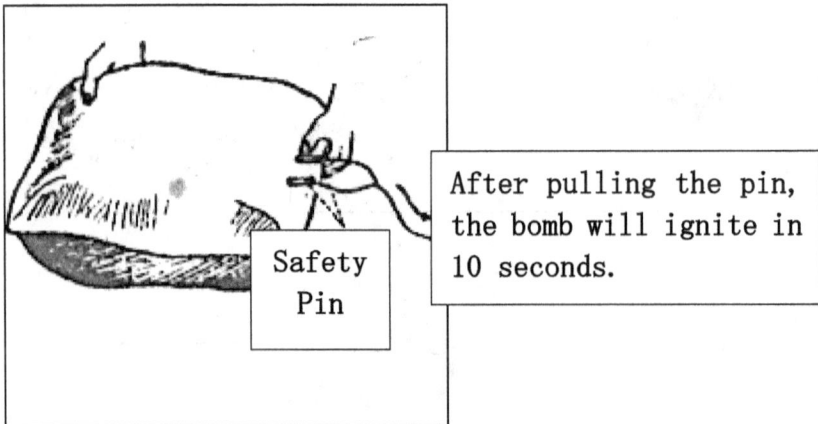

Safety
Pin

After pulling the pin,
the bomb will ignite in
10 seconds.

Example of a 3-Person Unit

Each team would have one Futon "pillow" bomb, one
bomb-tipped spear, two hand-thrown explosives, two
Molotov cocktails and seven hand grenades.
In addition, they would be equipped with wrapped
explosives to use as a Quick-Made bomb or mine.

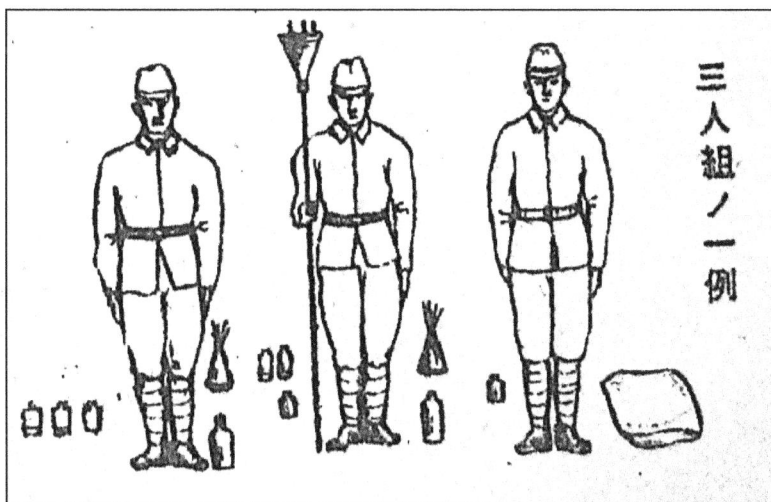

Newspaper Article 2
Well-Practiced Volunteer Attack Units

4. How to Carry Out an Attack

4. How to Carry Out an Attack

Your movements must be completely covert, thus it is imperative you remain concealed and not be discovered until the moment of your attack. When attacking do not rush and do not get flustered.

- If using a hand-thrown bomb, be sure to wait in a concealed place, perpendicular to your target, so you can throw at the side of the tank.
- When throwing a Molotov cocktail, to ensure it ignites with maximum power. Target the exhaust port near the engine on the back of the tank.
- When attacking with a bomb-tipped spear, use the same Kiai, shout unifying body and action, as you slam into your target with your whole body.
- When using a Futon "pillow" bomb, aim for the back of the tank and throw it down hard from a high place.

No matter which way you attack, remain calm and be certain to pull the safely pin. Do not lose a great chance to destroy the enemy.

4 攻撃・實施

1 手投爆雷（安全栓ヲ抜ク　ノヲ忘レルナ）

2 刺突爆雷

3 フトン爆雷

火焔瓶

火焔瓶コノ
コガヨイ

眞横カ
ラ投ゲ
ルコト

4. How to Carry Out an Attack
1. Hand-Thrown Bombs
2. Molotov Cocktail
(Do not forget to pull the safety pin)

Throw directly at the side.

This is the best place to throw the Molotov cocktail.

2. Bomb-tipped spear

3. Futon "Pillow" Bomb

5. How to Support a Close Quarter Attack on a Tank

Look for places that will allow you to hide yourself from the machineguns and submachineguns and shoot at the foot soldiers, eliminating them.

Use that opportunity to launch a close quarters attack.

Fire the grenade launcher from a place that cannot be seen. The grenades should arch down onto the foot soldiers accompanying the tank.

Newspaper Article 3
Our Ever-Victorious Military Strategy

1. *Teishin Kirikomi*
Volunteer Attack Units

1. *Teishin Kirikomi*
Volunteer Attack Units

The *Teishin Kirikomi*, Volunteer Attack Units, are a glorious reflection of the Imperial Army, which is renowned all over the world for its style of fighting. Our officers and men, have spread the blazing red fires of war and caused the blood of our enemies to hemorrhage all over the battlefields throughout Asia. The threat of our Volunteer Attack Units will be demonstrated with the unification of the triple threat of sniper fire, throwing hand grenades and close-quarters combat.

Newspaper Article 3
Our Ever-Victorious Military Strategy

2. *Sogeki* A Sniper

2. *Sogeki* A Sniper

The highest goal of a sniper is to always hit your target with the first shot. It requires that you adapt to the terrain and the disposition of the enemy when shooting. This is no different from the fundamentals taught during basic rifle training.

It goes without saying that your likelihood of hitting your target increases the closer you are to the enemy. Thus, you need to advance closer than 300 meters from your target before calmly sighting in.

If the enemy is prone, then aim for the chest. If standing then aim for the lower abdomen. If your target is a soldier parachuting, aim 2.5 body lengths below. This means to sight in one and a half body lengths below his legs.

二、狙撃

1 姿勢

立チ射チ應用

膝射チ

伏射チ

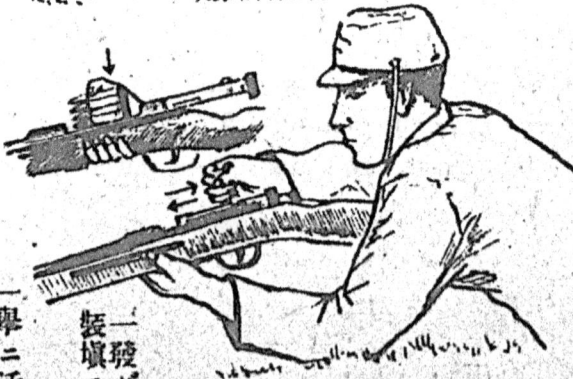

弾丸込メ

一擧ニ彈丸ノ根
本ヲ押シ込ム

一擧ニ活潑ニ
操作スルコト

一發ヅツ
裝塡スル

2. *Sogeki*
A Sniper

Shooting Postures

Useful when shooting while standing

Knee Shooting

Shooting While Lying Prone

Loading Bullets

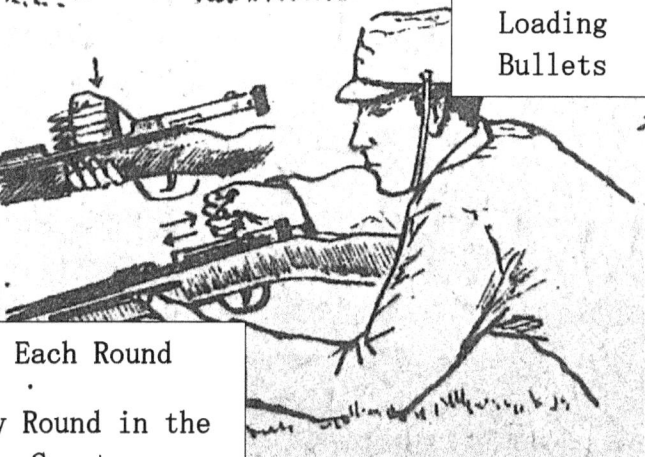

Push the clip of bullets entirely into the rifle.

Chamber Each Round

Make Every Round in the Clip Count

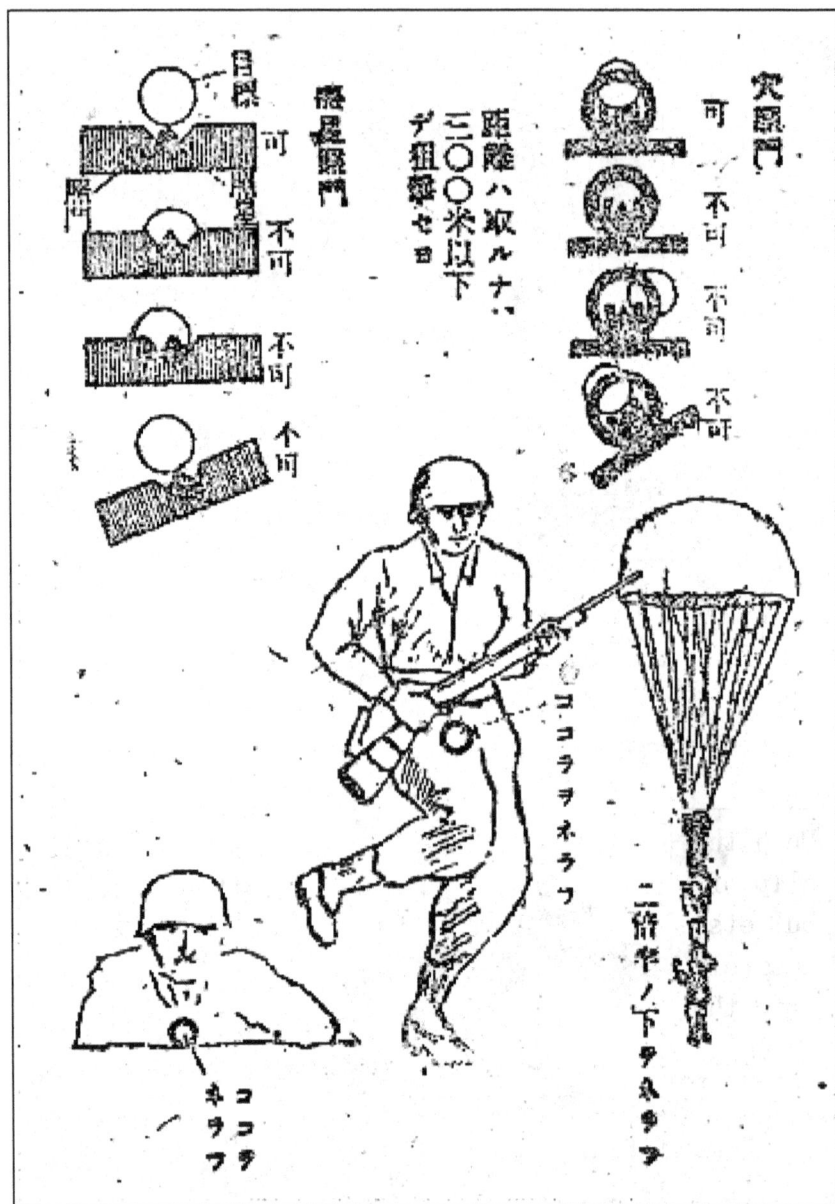

Using an 穴照門 Aperture Sight

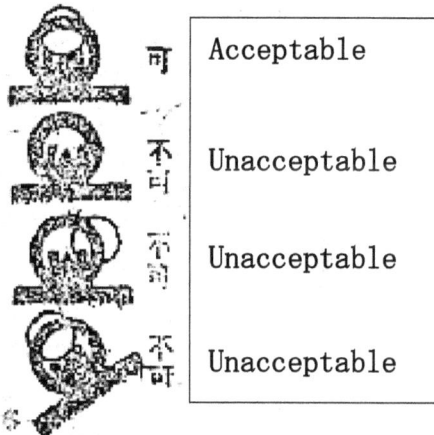

可	Acceptable
不可	Unacceptable
不可	Unacceptable
不可	Unacceptable

Comparing the Star, Comparing the Gate :
Using a Notch Sight

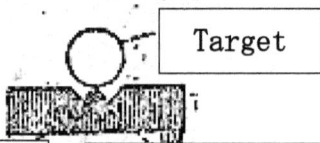

Target

"Comparing the Gate"
Rear Sight

"Comparing the Star"
Front Sight

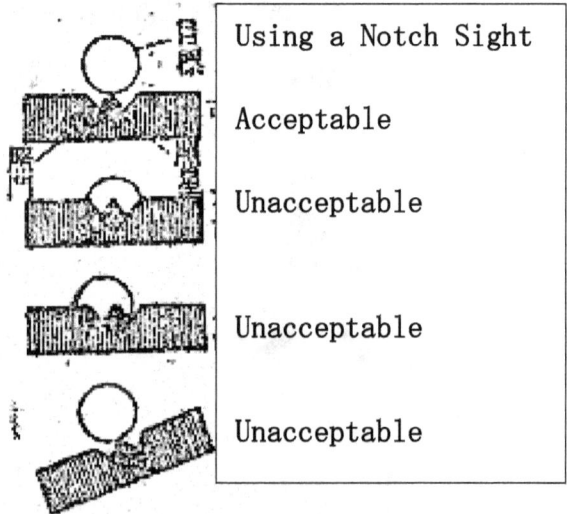

Using a Notch Sight

Acceptable

Unacceptable

Unacceptable

Unacceptable

Newspaper Article 3
Our Ever-Victorious Military Strategy

3. *Shuryudan Toteki*
Throwing Grenades

3. *Shuryudan Toteki*
Throwing Grenades

A grenade weighs 170 Monme, 637 grams. The standard grenade is effective up to 7 meters and there are also ones with handles. Empty bottles and cans can also be adapted.

To operate a grenade, first pull the safety pin and confirm the fuse is lit. Next, consider your throwing ability based on your everyday training. Third, throw while focusing all your power on one small point.

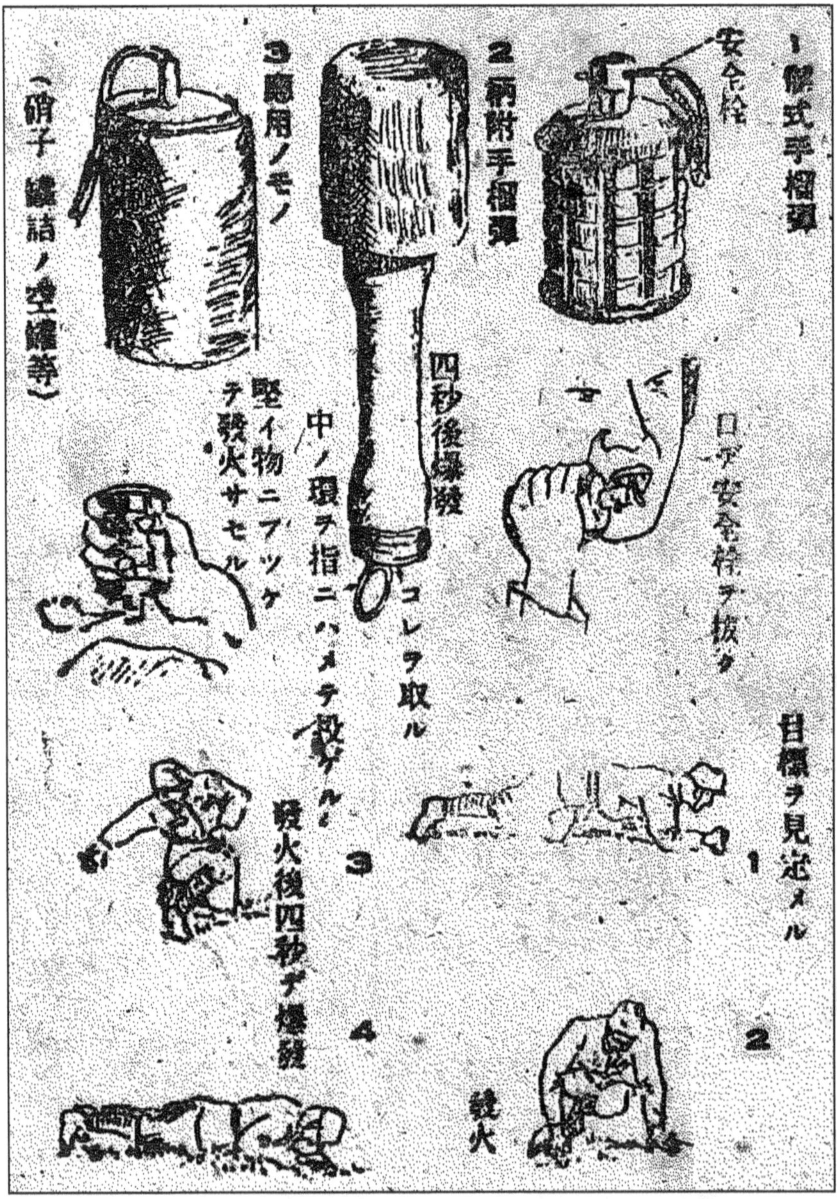
1 擲式手榴彈
安全栓
2 柄附手榴彈
3 應用ノモノ
（硝子 罐詰ノ空罐等）
口デ安全栓ヲ拔ク
四秒後爆發
コレヲ取ル
中ノ環ヲ指ニハメテ投ゲル
堅イ物ニブツケテ發火サセル
目標ヲ見定メル
1
2
發火
3
4
發火後四秒デ爆發

1. 九七式手榴弾 *Kyunana-shiki Shuryudan*
Type 97 Hand Grenade

Safety Pin

Pull the safety pin out with your teeth.

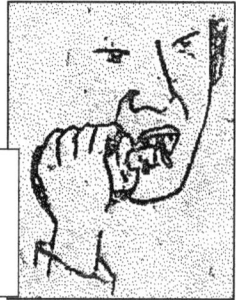

Strike against a hard surface to ignite.

2. Grenade with Handle

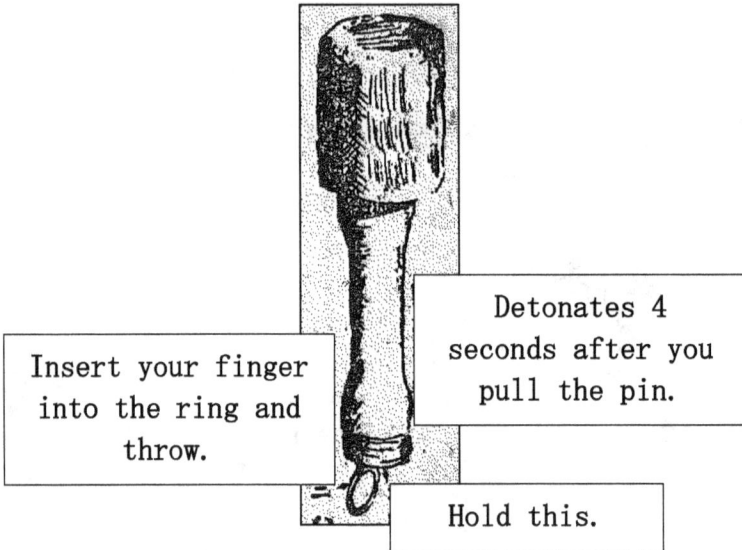

Insert your finger into the ring and throw.

Detonates 4 seconds after you pull the pin.

Hold this.

3. Adapted Object
(These can be glass bottles or cans filled [with explosives])

3. The grenade will explode 4 seconds after ignition.

1. Identify your target.

2. Ignite.

4.

Newspaper Article 3
Our Ever-Victorious Military Strategy

4. *Hakuhei Sento, Kakuto*
Close-Quarters Combat, Unarmed Fighting

國民抗戦必携

われらの必殺戦法 ③

4. *Hakuhei Sento, Kakuto*
Close-Quarters Combat, Unarmed Fighting

The best way to attack the tall Yankees in close-quarters combat with a sword is to use Tsuki, a straight thrust. Unless you are particularly skilled with a sword, cutting straight down from above or using a sweeping cut will not deliver a fatal blow.

Even if you don't have a Katana or spear, a sickle, hatchet, hammer, kitchen knife or picaroon, can all be used as a military weapon for a surprise attack.

If you come across an enemy moving about on his own, it will be easy to approach him from behind and then strike a fatal blow. It is best to use a sickle with a handle 3 Shaku, 90 centimeters long.

If you become engaged in hand to hand combat, the enemy will be attacking from above, so drop your hips down and strike to Mizo Ochi, the solar plexus, or kick to Kogan, the groin. In this situation make use of the striking and grappling techniques particular to the martial arts of Japan, such as those found in Judo or Karate.

No matter what you do, leaping in and sacrificing your body will result in victory.

四、白兵戰鬪、格鬪

1 刀 槍

背ノ高イヤン
キー共ノ腹ヲ
突ケ、斬ルナ、
ハラフナ

2 鎌、ナタ、玄能
出刃包丁、蔦口

後カラ奇襲セヨ

3 格鬪

其ノ他柔道、尉手
ノ手ヲ用フル

睪丸ヲ
蹴ル

水落チ
ヲ突ク

Our Ever-Victorious Military Strategy

4. *Hakuhei Sento, Kakuto*
Close-Quarters Combat, Unarmed Fighting

1. Using a Katana or Spear

Stab the Yankees, who tend to be tall, in the stomach. Don't try to cut, don't try to attack with a sweeping cut.

2. You should sneak up from behind and attack
unexpectedly using any of the following:

Kama Sickle
Nata Chopping hatchet
Genno Hammer
Deba-bocho Japanese-style Kitchen Knife
Tobiguchi Picaroon

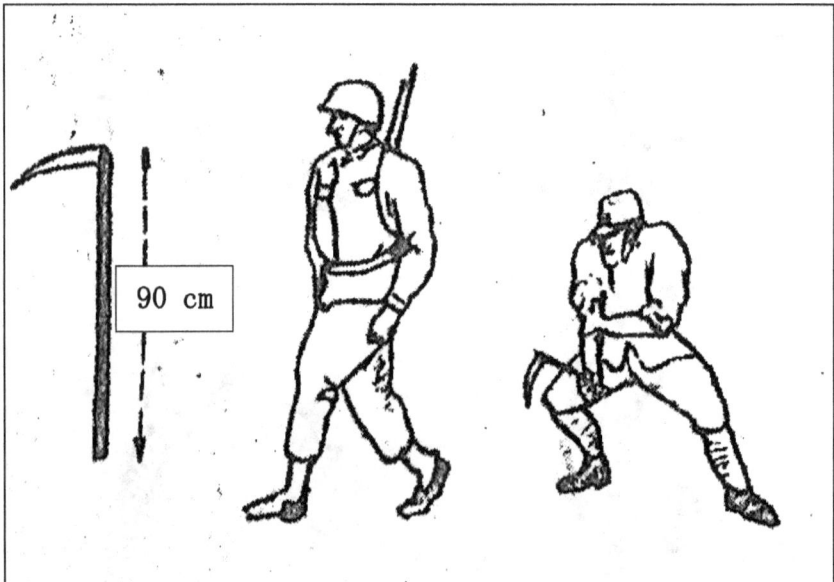

90 cm

3. Hand to Hand Fighting

Punch to Mizo-uchi "Water Drop" or the solar plexus.

Kick to Kogan, the testicles. In addition you can use Judo or Karate techniques.

Newspaper Article 4
Completely Committed to Operating Covertly

5. *Teishin Kirikomi*
Volunteer Attack Units

5. *Teishin Kirikomi*

Volunteer Attack Units

This describes how those that have become *Teishin Kirikomi,* Volunteer Attack Units, will advance on and invariably kill the arrogant enemy. Your entire body should be brimming with determination and composed courage, which you will use to uproot the enemy's military power. Thus, depending on the situation, you will have to respond quickly and deftly. You must be prepared to strive with all your might and take decisive action in order to achieve your mission.

1. How to Form a Unit, Items to be Carried

When you receive orders from your area leader, bear in mind that you have been selected to carry out a particular mission covertly and in complete secrecy. The members of the 3-person team should carry the following:

A gun or Katana, bamboo spear, picaroon or other such weapon.

In addition, grenades, Futon "pillow" bombs, explosives and armor piercing explosives (These come in two shapes, half-sphere and cone-shaped,) in addition to Molotov cocktails and other such weapons. You should also carry a map, a glow-in-the-dark compass, a whistle, a flashlight and a pair of pruning shears. In addition, each person should carry a water bottle and 2 or 3 days' worth of food.

五、挺身斬込

1 組ノ編成、携行資材

三人組

長ノ選定、指揮要領
ニ注意セヨ

同右 同右 小銃(又ハ刀、竹槍、蔦口)

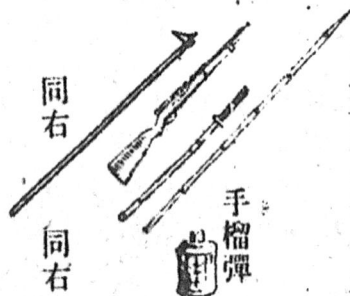

同右 同右 手榴彈

マッチ

爆藥

地圖

夜光羅針

破甲爆雷
（半球形、圓錐形）

フトン爆藥

火熖瓶

笛

懐中電燈

右ノ外水筒、糧食
各人二ー三日分

木バサミ

A 3-Person Unit

Be sure to follow the selection and operational parameters dictated by the overall leader.

Each person should be armed with a small gun.

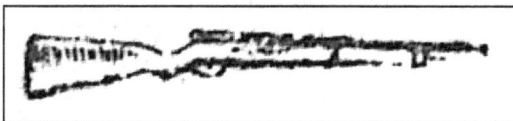

(Other options are a Katana,

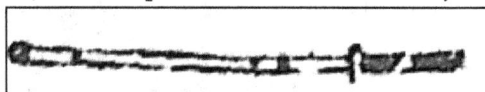

Takeyari Bamboo Spear,

or a *Tobiguchi* Picaroon.)

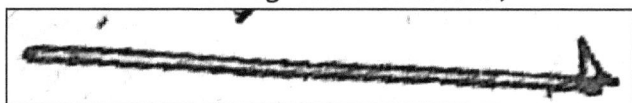

手榴彈	*Shuryudan* Grenade
マッチ	*Macchi* Matches
爆藥	*Bakuyaku* Explosives
フトン爆藥	*Futon Bakuyaku* Futon Explosive
破甲爆雷	*Hakou Bakurai* Armor shattering bomb. (Can be half-sphere or cone-shaped.)
地圖	*Chizu* Map
夜光羅針	*Yakorashin* Glow-in-the-dark compass

笛	*Fue* Whistle
懐中電燈	*Kaichu Dento* Pocket Flashlight
火焔瓶	*Kaenbin* Molotov Cocktail
木バサミ	*Kibasami* Pruning Shears
右ノ外水筒、糧食各人二―三日分	In addition to the items listed on this page, each person should have a water bottle and two or three days' worth of food.

Newspaper Article 4
Completely Committed to Operating Covertly

2. *Chikei Chibutsu no Riyo*
How to Use the Terrain and Man-made or Natural Features

2. *Chikei Chibutsu no Riyo*
How to Use the Terrain and Man-made or Natural Features

All of your activities will be done amongst the enemy, so you cannot allow even the slightest error.
A drainage ditch or flooded rice field that no one is likely to pass by is a road that is heaven sent for volunteer attack units. Finding a road that is not actually a road is a great boon, however if you encounter a smaller enemy unit that is not your primary target, remember to not allow a minor distraction to derail your main objective. You need to be single-minded in your determination to obliterate your target.

2 地形地物ノ利用

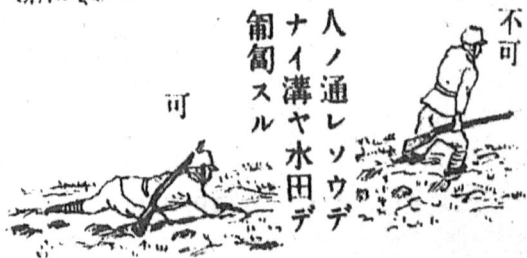

可

不可

可

不可

可

不可

可

不可

人ノ通レソウデ
ナイ溝ヤ水田デ
匍匐スル

可

不可

Good

Bad

Good

Bad

Bad

Good

Crawl through a water-filled rice field or drainage ditch that people are unlikely to pass near.

Good

Bad

Good

Bad

Newspaper Article 4
Completely Committed to Operating Covertly

3. *Hakai Shoiho*
How to Destroy or Incinerate

國民抗戰必携

決死必成の隠密行

3 破壊焼却法

1、組の編成、携行

材料

五、挺身斬込

2、地形地物の利用

可

不可

3. *Hakai Shoiho*
How to Destroy or Incinerate

1. To destroy mortars, throw two or more grenades down the barrel. Also break the sighting mechanism located on the legs.
2. To destroy artillery you will need between 2-8 kilograms of explosives depending on the size of the weapon. Blow up the most fragile part, the barrel. Also destroy the sighting mechanism.
3. When attacking a large bore cannon, pack between 8-10 kilograms of explosives into the tail end, place a Futon bomb on the body and use a bomb-tipped spear on the barrel to destroy each part of the weapon.
4. To destroy fuel barrels, throw a grenade or start a fire with a match after opening a hole.
5. For boxes of explosives, use three or more grenades to start an explosion that will spread to the rest.
6. Throw a grenade into a tent to kill all the enemy soldiers inside at once.
7. Incinerate military provisions by igniting sticks, dry grass or other flammable material.
8. Use scissors to cut communication and other wires. However, if you continue this activity for too long, you are likely to be discovered. You should judge the situation carefully before deciding on a course of action.

３ 破壊燒夷法

１ 迫撃砲
手榴弾砲口ニ
二ケ以上
入レ
照準具ヲ打
チ壊ス

２ 火砲
爆薬
二—八キロ
照準具ヲ
一打チ壊ス

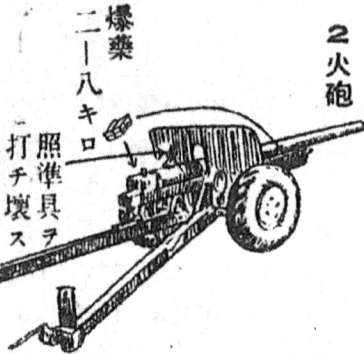

３ 大口徑砲
刺突
爆雷

爆雷

フトン
爆雷
八—十キロ

戦車ハフトン爆雷
ガ良イ

爆薬

４ ドラム罐
手榴弾
マッチデ火ヲツケル

５ 弾薬
手榴弾
三ケ中
ヘ入レ

８ 週信線切断

６ 天幕
手榴弾

７ 糧食
柴、枯草デ放火

Strike and break the sighting instrument.

1 迫撃砲

手榴弾砲口ニ二ケ以上入レル

1. *Hakugekiho* Mortar
Place two or more grenades in the barrel.

Use 2-8 Kilograms of explosives.

Strike and break the sighting instrument

2 火砲

2. *Kaho* Cannon

Use a Futon bomb.

Use 8-10 Kilograms of explosives. It is best to use Futon explosives on tanks.

爆刺
雷突

３大口径砲

6

3. *O-guchi Keiho*
Large-Bore Cannon

Use a bomb-tipped spear.

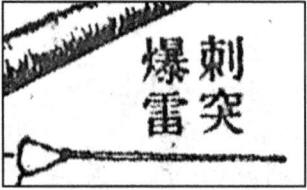

爆刺
雷突

Grenade **4 ドラム罐** Match	4. *Dorumukan* Fuel Barrels Use a grenade or light it with a match.
5 弾薬 ルヘ三手入ケ榴レ中彈	5. *Bakuyaku* Explosives Put three grenades inside.
6 天幕 Grenade	6. *Tenmaku* Tent
柴、枯草デ放火 **7 糧食**	7. *Ryoshoku* Food Storage Make a fire with sticks or dried grass.
8 通信線切断	8. *Tsushinsen Setsudan* Cut communication wires

Newspaper Article 5
Seizing the Chance:
Adapting to the Requirements of the Moment

4. *Machibuse Yugeki* Ambushes and Raids

4. *Machibuse Yugeki*
Ambushes and Raids

Overview
Members of Volunteer Attack Units should not solely follow their directive to launch surprise attacks on enemy positions. During the course of your mission, if you see a chance to strike the enemy that will result in great damage, you should take decisive action. Thus commanders are very much in favor of units acting on targets of opportunity that may present themselves.

4. *Machibuse Yugeki*
Ambushes and Raids

1. Attacking a Unit

A small force attacking a group of enemy soldiers, throwing them into confusion as you kill them can only be achieved by a surprise attack using an unconventional plan.

For example, setting up a base of operations near a road cut through a mountain, a bridge near a village or in the woods and keeping watch will allow you to decimate the enemy. Using automatic weapons to fire on the enemy in a pincer's movement is best.

Further, if you are on top of a cliff you can drop lumber or chunks of earth down on the enemy. This shows that primitive fighting methods can be effective. When doing this, consider the convoy's speed and drop material in front of them to stop the column. Then dump more material on them like an avalanche. This will kill or wound all those riding in the convoy.

2. Make Use of the Enemy's Inattention

In order to sneak into the midst of the enemy, it is first necessary to overcome several security nets.

In particular, as you approach your objective, no doubt you will soon encounter scouts on patrol as well as enemy guards. Attack when you find an opportune moment, and strike them down.

In other words, if you find a solitary enemy who is inattentive, stab him to death from behind, or cut him down with one sword cut, splitting him cleanly into two parts. If the enemy is unaware anyone is behind him, particularly if it is an officer or man armed with a machine gun, then such an important individual should be killed with sniper fire.

Further, if the enemy is formed into a small unit, then the explosion of a hand grenade will kill them all.

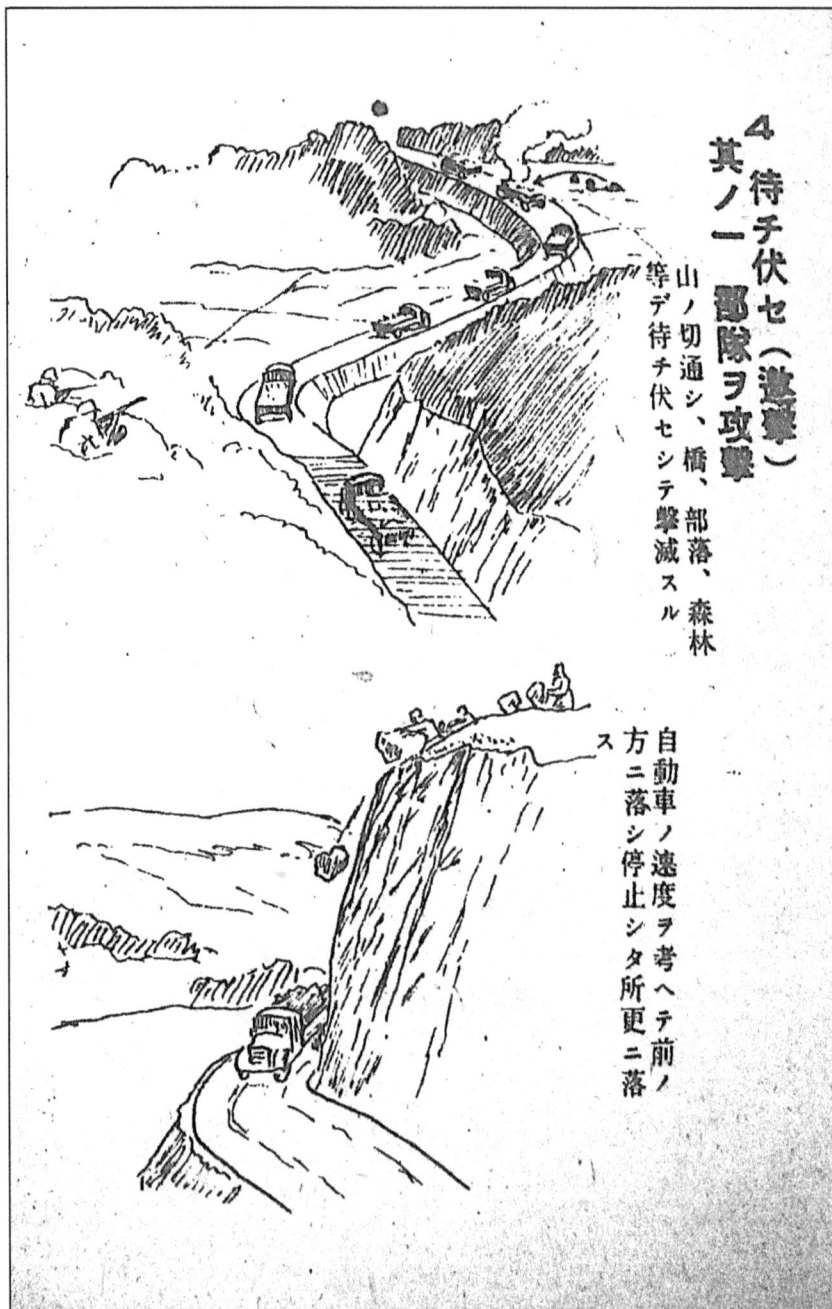

４　待チ伏セ（邀撃）

其ノ一　部隊ヲ攻撃

山ノ切通シ、橋、部落、森林
等デ待チ伏セシテ撃滅スル

自動車ノ速度ヲ考ヘテ前ノ
方ニ落シ停止シタ所更ニ落
ス

Wait where the road cuts through the mountains, near a bridge, a small village, forest or other such place and cut them down.

Consider the speed a vehicle is moving and drop objects in front. When the vehicles stop, drop more.

其ノ二 敵ノ油断ニ乗ズ

敵ガ一人ナラバ後カラ刺シ（斬リ）殺セ

敵ガ後ニモ居タラバ重要ナ者（將校、機關銃手ナド）ヲ狙撃セヨ

多勢カタマツテ居タラバ手榴彈ヲ投ゲヨ

イヅレニセヨ攻撃迄見ツカラヌコト

後ニ敵ガ
居ラヌ時

將校

If the enemy is alone then kill him by stabbing (cutting) him from behind.

When the enemy does not think anyone is behind him.

If you can see the backs of the enemy and there is an important person there (an officer, a machine gun operator and so on) then try to snipe him.

Officer

If there is a large group in close formation then throw a grenade.
No matter what you do, ensure that you are not discovered before you attack.

Newspaper Article 6
Obliterate Enemy Camps in One Stroke

5. Volunteer Attack Units
Part One : General Outline

5. Volunteer Attack Units
Part One : General Outline

As was previously mentioned your activities and movements should be completely covert, however as you enter the area of your target, the enemy stronghold, it goes without saying that you need to absolutely be on your highest possible guard.

The fact that the enemy uses foot patrols, military guard dogs, loudspeakers, along with all manner of barbed wire and other equipment, was all seen on the islands in the south seas. This was not just in the Philippines but also seen in all operations in Burma and other places.

To give a general outline:
1. Don't use roads
2. Once you have infiltrated behind enemy lines, carefully observe the enemy.
3. Keeping an eye out for roving patrols, decide on the place you will launch your attack.
4. Commit to your method of attack
5. Withdraw and split up, with each member moving on their own. Meet back at a pre-arranged spot.
It is more effective to implement your plan at night.

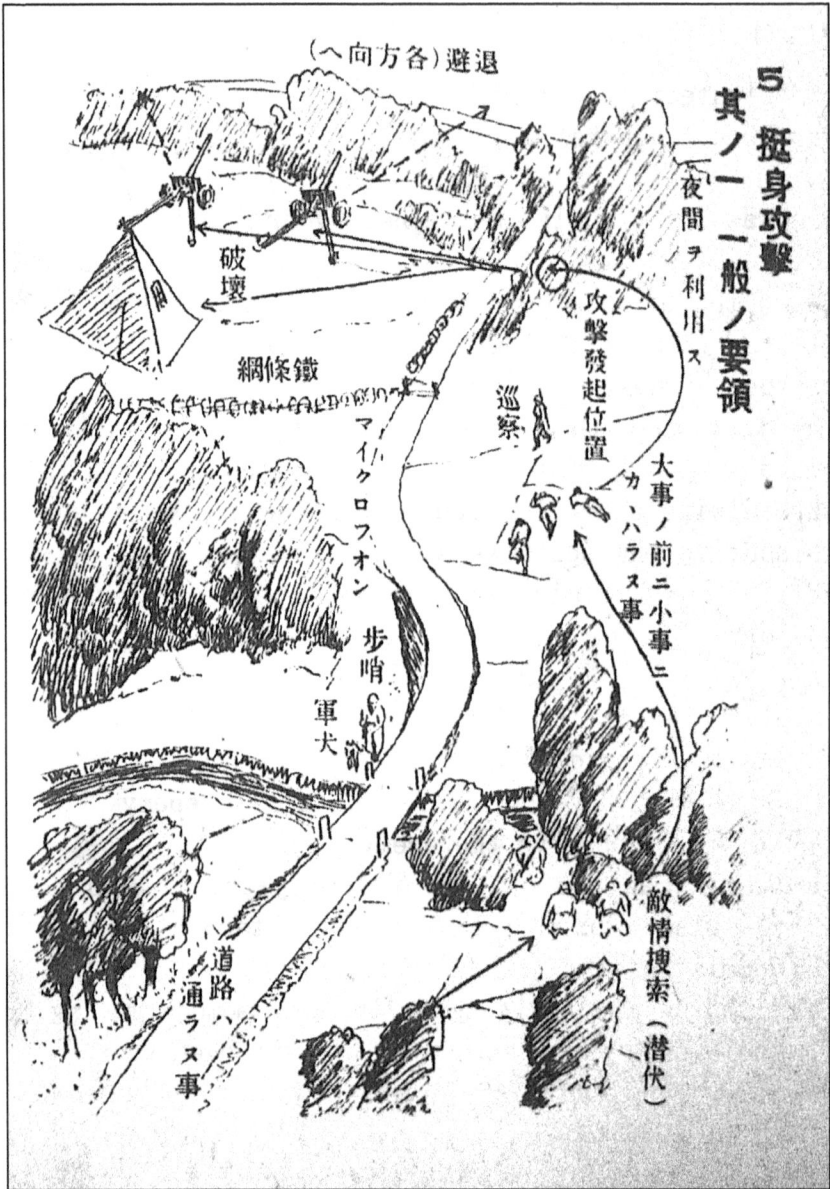

Part One: General Outline

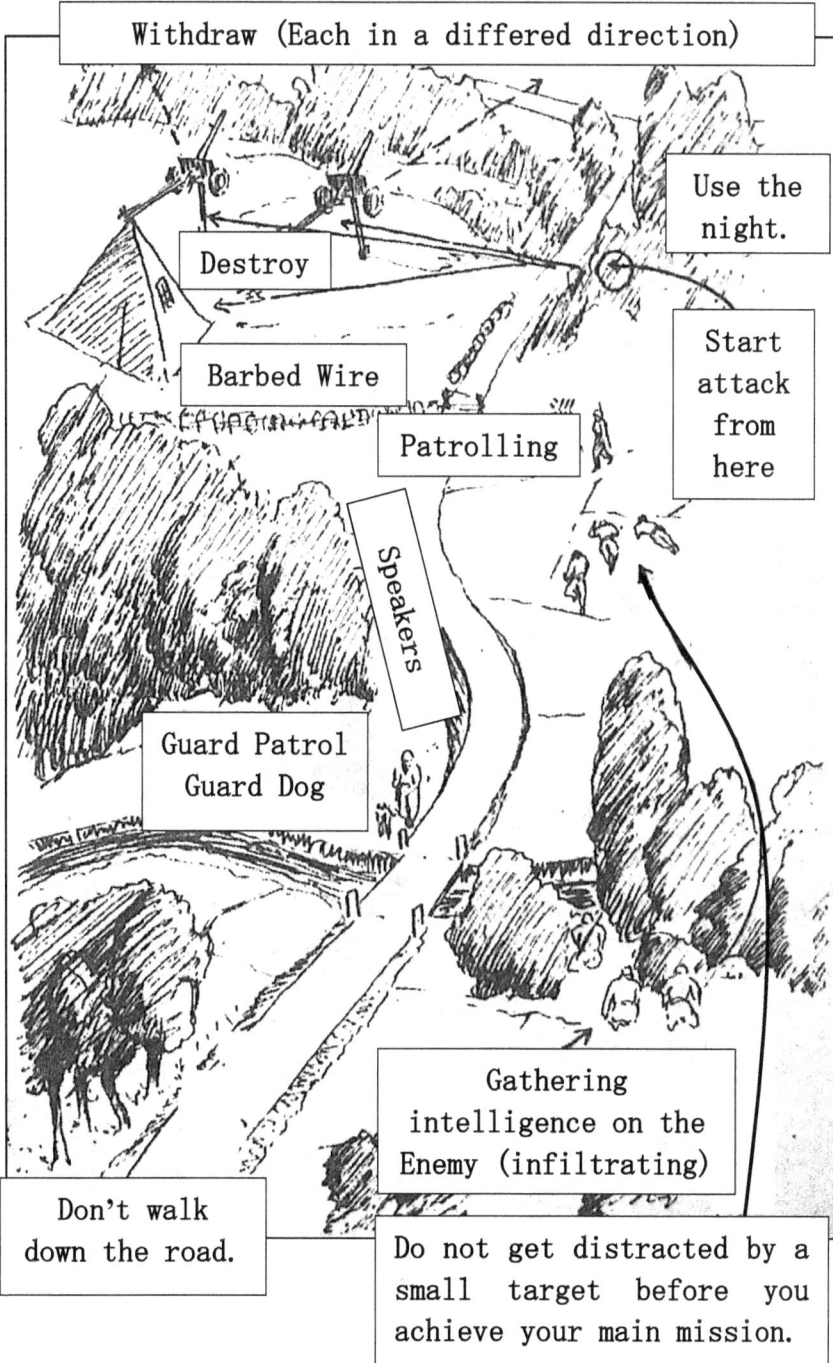

Newspaper Article 6
Obliterate Enemy Camps in One Stroke

Part Two
Draw the enemy's attention in one direction before attacking from another.

Part Two
Draw the enemy's attention in one direction before attacking from another.

Even though this is a "cutting in" attack it does not deviate from the fundamentals of battle. There is the true focus of your attack and the false attack which you use to distract. As history teaches us, when crafting this strategy there are a thousand variations of 10,000 possible approaches.
For example, one member of a group can blow up some fuel barrels sewing confusion in the enemy. While they are concentrating on that disturbance the main force takes a different route and blows up airplanes or another important objective.
This is how Volunteer Attack Units complete their mission as ordered.

其ノ二　敵ノ注意ヲ一方ニ引キツケテ他方カラ攻撃

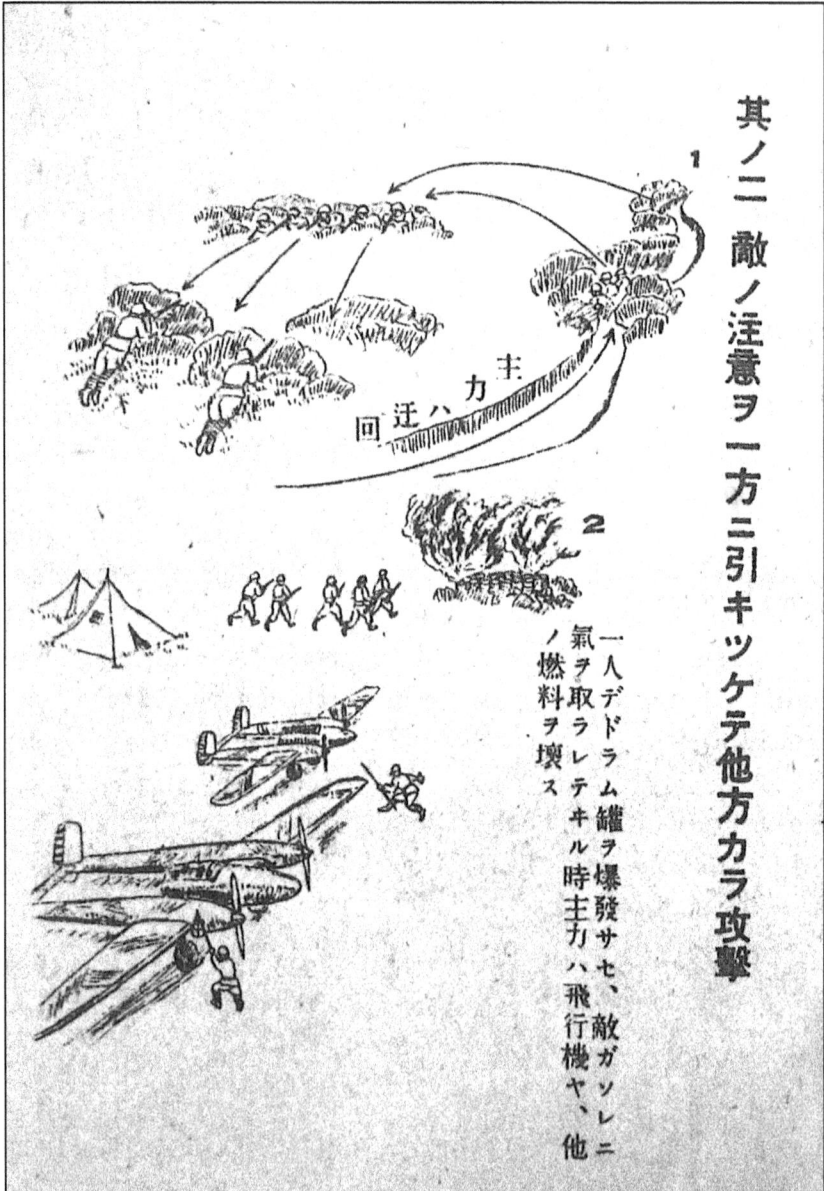

1

主力ハ迂回

2

一人デドラム罐ヲ爆發サセ、敵ガソレニ氣ヲ取ラレテキル時主力ハ飛行機ヤ、他ノ燃料ヲ壊ス

Part Two : Draw the enemy's attention in one direction while you launch your assault in another.

1. The main force should take an alternate route.

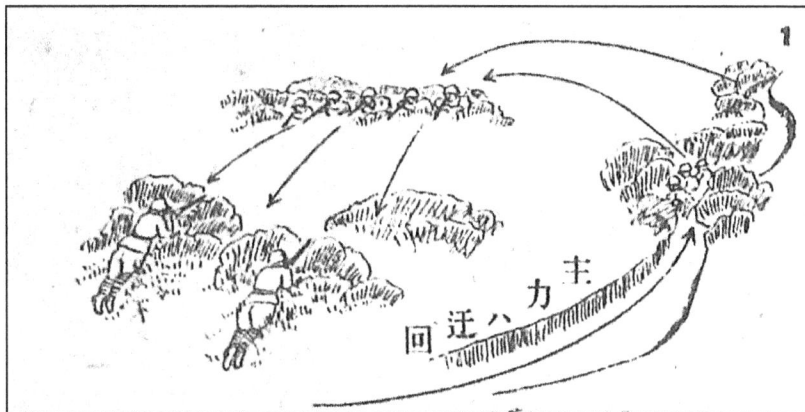

2. Have one person blow up some barrels of fuel. While the enemy is busy dealing with that, your main force attacks airplanes or other fuel storage tanks.

Newspaper Article 6
Obliterate Enemy Camps in One Stroke

Part Three
Attacking from multiple directions at the same time.

一擧に敵陣を覆滅

國民抗戰必携

Part Three
Attacking from multiple directions at the same time.

Volunteer Attack Units do not devote all their energy solely to assaulting their main objective, rather they decimate the enemy's fighting strength at every turn. Stories of the Volunteer Attack Units in Guadalcanal have already been widely reported which caused the blood of a hundred-million citizens to go wild. Thus we should emulate that model as we face the coming autumn.

其ノ三　各方面同時攻撃

一ツダケデ満足スルナ

Part Three: Attacking from multiple directions at the same time.

Don't be satisfied with just one!

Newspaper Article 7
Obliterating Airborne Units Requires Fast and Decisive Action

1. *Shogaibutsu* : Obstacles

1. *Shogaibutsu*: Obstacles

Areas that are considered to have a high likelihood of being the target of airborne assault should, if ordered to by the military, take measures to obstruct their landing.

On large roads, construct a series of irregularly placed and angled wooden stakes in combination with mines. On flat areas place wooden cards, rocks and lumber to prevent gliders from being able to land successfully.

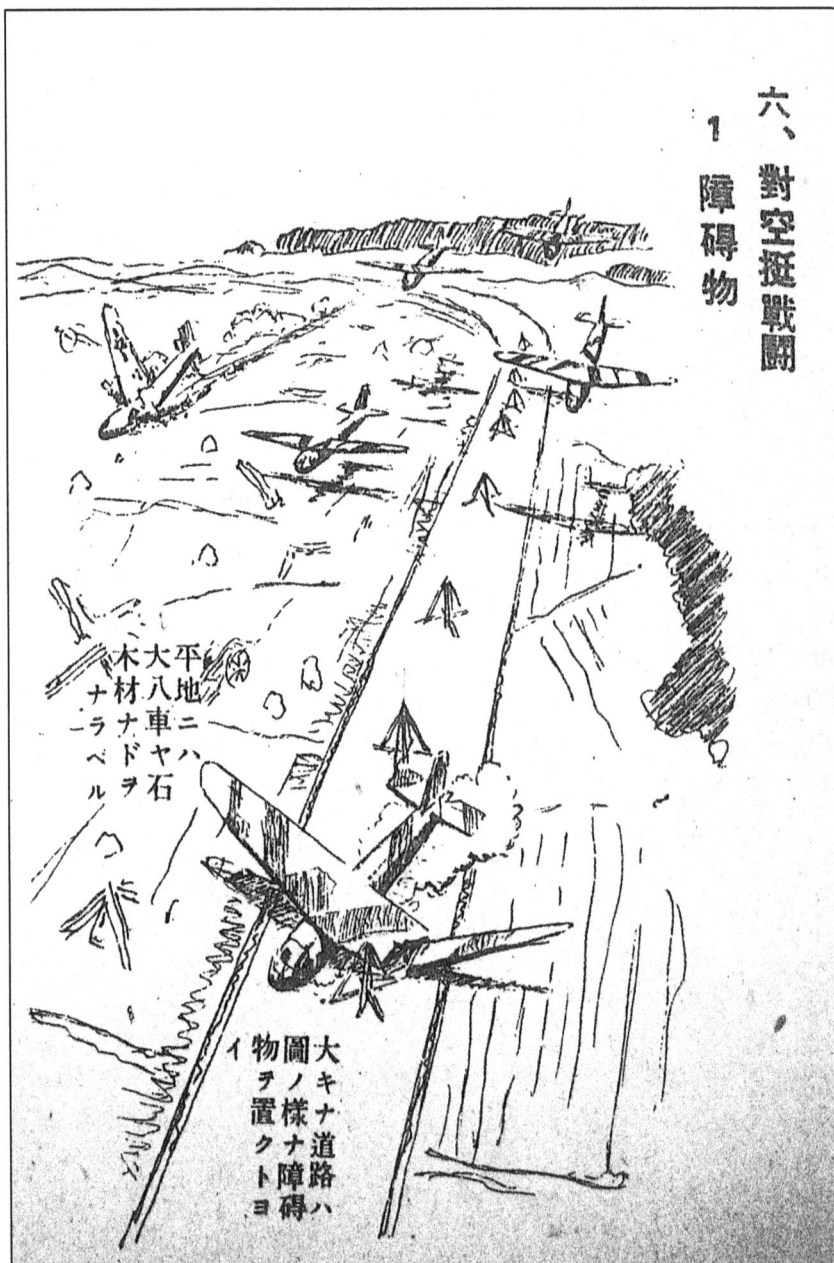

Six, Fighting Against Military Aircraft
1. *Shogaibutsu*
Obstacles

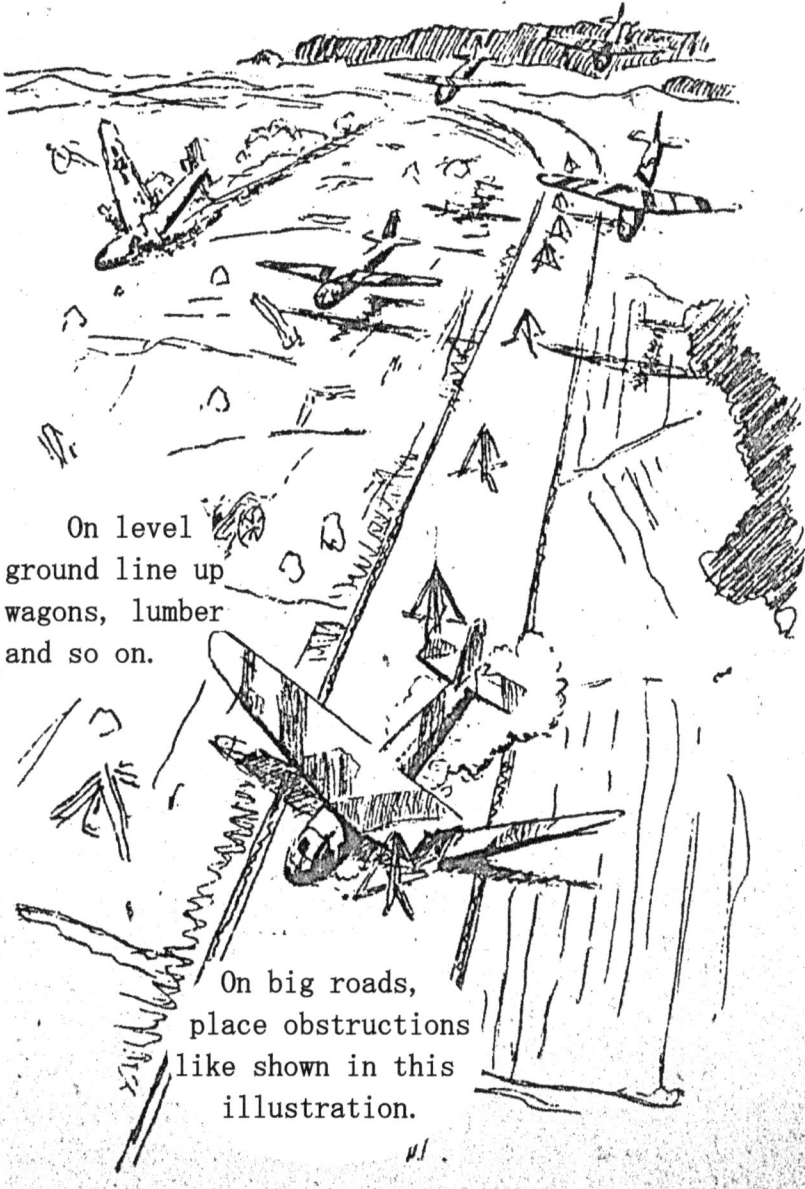

On level ground line up wagons, lumber and so on.

On big roads, place obstructions like shown in this illustration.

Newspaper Article 7
Obliterating Airborne Units Requires Fast and Decisive Action

2. General knowledge regarding fighting against airborne units

2. General knowledge regarding fighting against airborne units

Looking at the enemy's military strategy it is clear that they will not rely solely on sending individual airborne units. It goes without saying the enemy will attack with its full explosive power using gun and bomb attacks to support their assault. We cannot hesitate in the face of this intense assault, but must remain firm and sweep the enemy soldiers away.

Next, the Inspectorate General of Military Training has prepared an illustrated guide outlining what actions need to be taken.

In order for us to obliterate the enemy's airborne infantry units we must all move quickly and in unison.

1. If tasked with observing you should not be afraid of the enemy's bombing attacks. You should observe accurately. If you see figures being dropped from aircraft, confirm that they are human. (The enemy may try to fool you with mannequins.)

2. When passing information, both the sender and receiver should do their duty and not allow any communications to be missed. Do not ignore any communications and do not panic.

3. Make your reports quickly and be sure to describe the scene and report the number and type of what you see. This type of reporting should be practiced beforehand.

4. If what you see matches an enemy target, then immediately attack it with ferocious intensity. Airborne troops are most vulnerable in the time before they touch the ground. Be daring and quick, even if you don't hit every target.

5. When building obstructions in an area the enemy is likely to land, make use of anything that may be at and don't concern yourself with a specific method of construction. Everyone should cooperate with military construction efforts.

6. Protect important places (bridges, storehouses, factories, train stations etc···) Defend your hometown, this is the way to save the nation.

In order to make emergency reports of enemy paratroopers, use fireworks, signal fires, smoke, radios, phones, pigeons, horses, bicycles or make your way on foot. The efforts you make, as shown in the illustrations, are our countermeasures.

Our Strategy 1

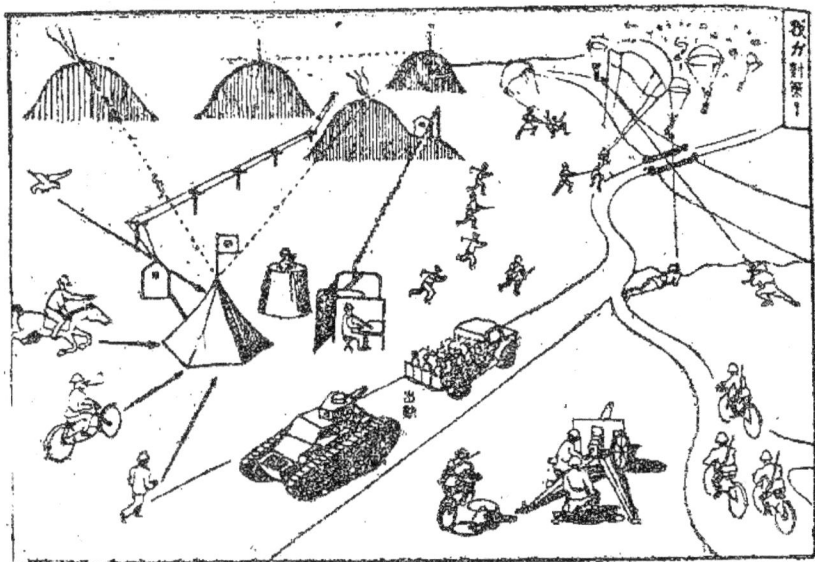

	Messenger Pigeon		Snipers
	Messenger on Horseback		
	Making announcements by bicycle.		
	Soldiers advancing by bicycle.		
	出勤 *Shukkin* Advancing		

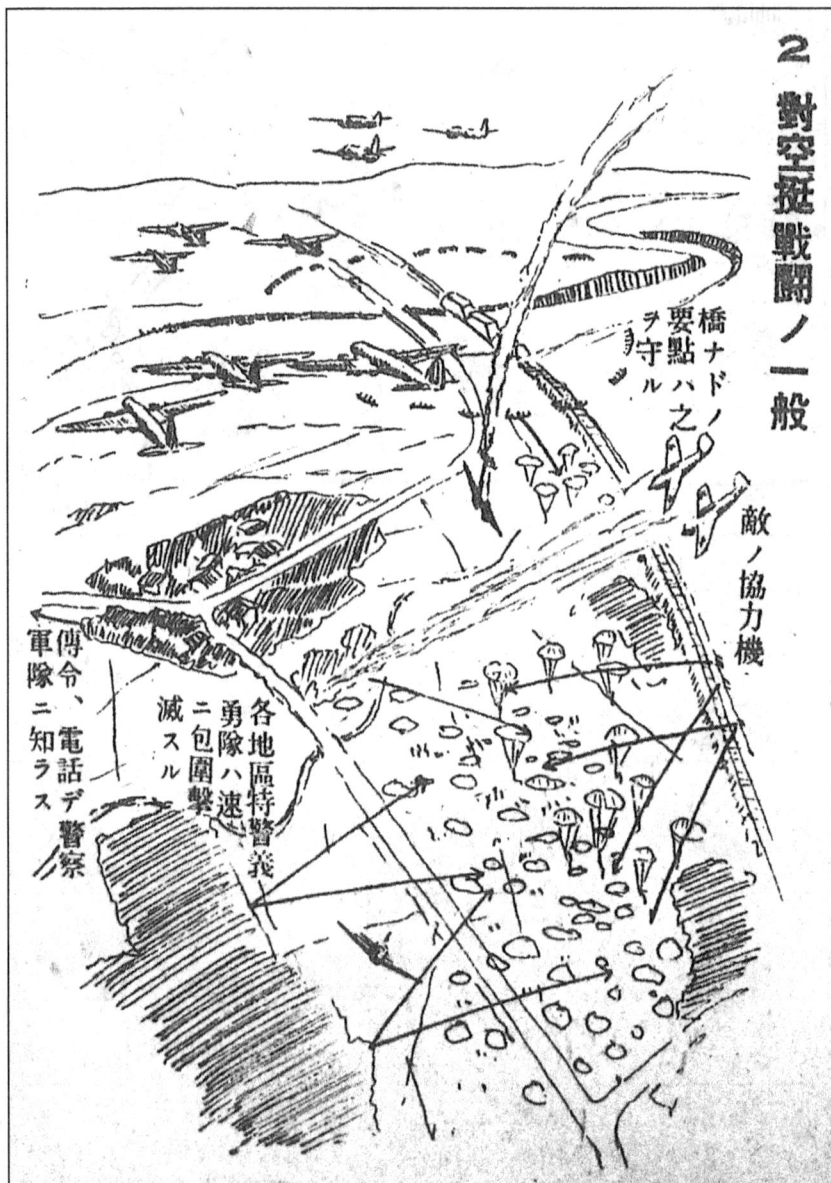

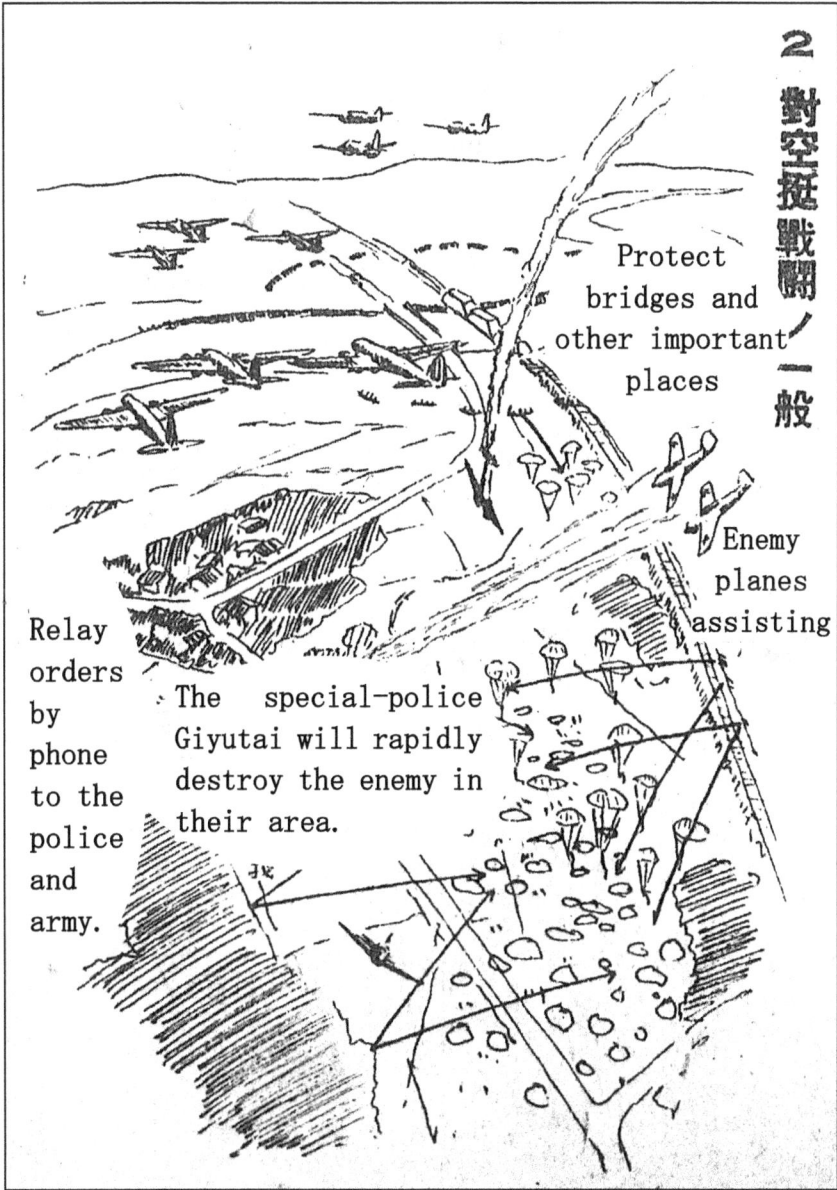

2 對空挺戦闘ノ一般

Protect bridges and other important places

Enemy planes assisting

Relay orders by phone to the police and army.

The special-police Giyutai will rapidly destroy the enemy in their area.

Newspaper Article 8
We Are Not Afraid of Anything

7.　Gas・Defending Against Flamethrowers

國民抗戰必攜

我ら何者も恐れず

七、瓦斯、火焰防護

In war, you need to be prepared for any situation. Setting aside the gas attacks for now, it is important to note that the American military makes extensive use of flamethrowers in land battles. This is particularly true when they attack encampments, as was seen in the battles on each of the southern islands.

No matter where you encounter it, the flamethrower will at first appear to be a weapon of astounding intensity, however if you remain calm and act properly there is nothing to fear.

1. Gas

If you have a mask that prevents poison gas then wear that. If not, then you can use a Tenugui, general purpose cloth, or a piece of gauze. Soak it in water and tie it around your mouth and nose, breathing slowly. At the same time try to move upwind and to a spot with higher elevation.

If liquid forms of mustard gas or Lewisite gas are being dropped like rain from above, then cover your body with cloth, oiled paper or straw. Move to a place that has not been exposed to the liquid and allow the gas to dissipate rather than trying to incinerate it. The characteristics of each are as follows.

Gas Weapons that Quickly Dissipate

Tear gas
1. If it coats your eyes, it will cause tears to flow
2. When the gas disperses, you will recover
You can completely protect yourself with a gas mask.
It is colorless or appears as a thin white colored vapor or smoke.

Sneezing Gas
1. Even if the gas is diffuse your nose and throat will begin to hurt and you will sneeze.
2. If the gas is thick and you breath it in, your chest will hurt and you will start to throw up.
3. Once the gas clears you will recover and return to your usual level of energy.
With a gas mask on you may still be able to smell the gas but you will not be adversely affected.
It is a colorless gas for the most part but may appear like greyish white smoke.

Suffocating Gas: Carbonyl Chloride

1. Breathing in the diffuse gas for a long period of time results in the same amount of damage as breathing in a dense gas for a short period of time.
2. If you breath in when the gas is thick around you, after two or three hours you will develop a cough. Breathing will become difficult and in severe cases can cause you to suffocate to death.
3. Be aware if you are in an area with diffuse gas. If you do not pay attention, or take preventive measures, you will end up breathing in a large dose.

A gasmask will completely protect you. The gas is usually colorless but can appear as a white vapor.

Gas Weapons That Linger

Poison Gas: Hydrogen Cyanide • Carbon Monoxide

1. If the gas is diffuse and you breath it in, your head will hurt and you will become dizzy.
2. If the gas is dense and you breath it in, you will be poisoned and die.

You can protect yourself with a gasmask.
1. You will not be injured if you are outside.
2. You can protect against carbon monoxide with a gasmask.

The former appears as a pale white or colorless vapor. The latter is a colorless and odorless vapor.

Blister Gas : Mustard Gas • Lewisite Gas

1. If the liquid gets on your skin, in 10 hours it will begin to become inflamed and blister.
2. If any of the above are in gas form they will damage the eyes. If inhaled, they can all damage the lungs.

When these are in liquid form they appear dark brown, however in gas form they are colorless.

七、瓦斯、火焔防護

1 瓦斯

瓦斯、火焔共ニ恐ルルナ
防毒面ガアレバソレヲ被ル

「マスク」ヤ手拭ニ、布ヤ「ガーゼ」
ヲ水ニヒタシテ掛ケ靜ニ呼吸スル

ナルベク風上、高イ所ヘ行ク事

「イペリット」ヤ「ルイサイト」ノ
雨下ノ場合ハ布ヤミノヲカブリ
急イデ毒化サレヌ所ヘ行ッテス
グ濯ノツイタモノハ燒キ捨テヨ

防毒面ガアレバソレヲ被ル

1. Do not be afraid of gas or flamethrowers.

If you have a gas-mask, wear that. You can make a mask out of a Tenugui, multipurpose towel, a piece of cloth or gauze. Soak it in water and tie it around your face. Breathe calmly and try to move upwind and to a higher elevation.

If mustard gas or lewisite is raining down, cover yourself with a piece of cloth or a straw raincoat. Move quickly to an area that has not been exposed to the poison and burn everything that the poison touched.

Newspaper Article 8
We Are Not Afraid of Anything

2. Defending Against Flamethrowers

國民抗戰必携 ⑧

我ら何者も恐れず

七、瓦斯、火焔防護

1、瓦斯

[一] 瓦斯

[二] 催涙瓦斯 誘導瓦斯（仮称）

2、火焔防護

2. Defending Against Flamethrowers

Fundamentally the flamethrower is a close-range weapon. If you understand the range the weapon can reach and use objects and land features to hide behind, you can take the user out with sniper fire. For example, even if flames from the weapon reach you, do not panic. Instead, pour water on a woven grass mat, or even pour water on a straw hat or a tent. Use that as a shield. Waiting for an opportunity, attack the flamethrower user from the side.

The fact that despite incendiary bombs being dropped on us, we emerged victorious, so a flamethrower is nothing in comparison.

２　火焔防護

火焔發射手ヲ物カゲカラ
狙ヒ撃チシテ殺ス

火焔ヲ吹キカケラレタラサワガ
ズ濡レムシロ、笠、天幕ナドデ
遮リ速ニ横ノ方カラ攻撃スル

2. Defending against a flame thrower

Shoot and kill the flamethrower operator from behind an obstruction.

When the flamethrower operator shoots fire, do not panic. Use a wet hat, tent and so on as a shield. Move quickly to the side and attack from there.

www.ingramcontent.com/pod-product-compliance
Lightning Source LLC
Chambersburg PA
CBHW050536280326
41933CB00011B/1602